Seeds

A Poetry Book

Casey Levi

BookLeaf
Publishing

India | USA | UK

Dedication

To my younger self

Preface

Love has the power to transform us in ways we never thought possible. It can lift us to euphoric heights and plunge us into the depths of despair. Through the journey of loving someone and losing yourself in the process, I discovered that sometimes, the greatest love story is the one we have with ourselves.

Acknowledgements

I would like to extend my heartfelt appreciation to all those who have taken the time to listen to me during my moments of heartbreak and have been there for me in my times of need. Your support and understanding have meant the world to me. I am truly grateful for your unwavering presence and for always seeing the good within me. Thank you for being such an important part of my life.

Autumn

In the midst of autumn on a cold night
Thy leaves rustle under stars so bright
A howl in the wind I pull my jacket tighter
Shallow shadows creep up thy walls
Fainted whispers, cackles, and calls
Walk amongst thy dead on thy hallows eve
We open thy door to creepy crawly things
A wicked smile on thy black lips
Our brews of potions we sip
Thou mustn't be afraid of the dark
Tis the season of thy witching hour
Gather around thy dying flowers
Beauty in the midst
We call her Autumn

Fall Mornings

It's that time again when the leaves begin to change.

The leaves once-darkened shades of forest green transition into vibrant hues of oranges, yellows, and rustic browns.

The oak trees smell misty with damp rain. Pull your hoodie tight and take a walk with me.

You take my hand and walk us towards the creek, the crunching of leaves beneath our feet.

On a late November day, the sun still peeks through the trees, and a cold chill settles in. We sit, reminiscing about the years we spent. Your rich laughter echoing against the mountain tops, you envelop me in your warmth.

We stayed long past midnight, a small lit fire crackling amid the night. Smells of roasted marshmallows and hot cocoa, could it be this simple? Just you and I waking up to these fall mornings?

Per Sempre

Your voice is like honey
So smooth and yummy
To lick your lips for just one taste
The time we have, I don't want to waste
From the start
You've had my heart
Travel back to the day we met
A day I'll never forget
Baby, there's no need to say
I'm only one call away
But if you ever need to hear me say
Just close your eyes and picture that day
A breath of fresh air and the warmth of the sun on your
face
There is no other love that can replace
Open your eyes to see my smile
Won't you kick back and stay awhile?
I'm down for you
Since day two
It's technically true

So come thru
Grab and hold me tight
We'll disappear out of sight
We only have this day
But you are my Per Sempre (Forever)

Sunday Afternoon

Lazy Sunday Afternoons
We were children laughing
Climbing trees and jumping in rivers
We never saw the clouds darken
When laughter turned silent
Our hearts parted
Some live fearless
How I envy them
Our ways parted, two separate paths
It was a lazy Sunday Afternoon
We climbed that tree
You took my hand,
Kissed me
And we jumped
But only one of us fell

Siren

An old dusty box where these memories used to lie
Shoved into the dark crevices of an attic floor
It was in the midst of a summer day in July
The hours ticking on that old grandfather clock
Words scribbled across these pages, nevermore
Take a walk down to the shore, we'll meet by the dock
Cold water rushing our lungs
Don't forget to hold your breath
And listen to the sea siren songs
An illusion of love, a fate far worse than death

Weightless

Today I woke to the sun shining through the cracked
curtains
A soft breeze through the summer air
Birds chirping away
My tired eyes I pry open
Your face across the screen
But not all was right in the world
The heaviness of your voice
A weight I cannot describe
These thoughts are no longer of pride, but hopelessness
Because no matter how much time goes by
You are there and I am here
Only seconds and then you were gone
The weight of your voice settling on my heart
We drift through this sunny summer day
Longing to be laid up
Would you press your lips to mine and pull me closer?
Your brown eyes reflecting
Speak into me

I'll take what is left
And we'll be weightless

Anxiety

Heart racing
Palms clammy
Throat tightening
These walls are closing in on me

Lungs collapsing
Body shaking
Teary-eyed
There is no escape from here

Morning Sorrows

The dreary clouds darkened my hazy day
Pulling the cotton covers around me
This chill to my bones
It is broken within me
Slowly killing what is left
Always a space of where you should be
But you will never see
If only I could wish one wish
Reach inside my chest
Grip onto my heart
Do you feel it constrict?
A shuddering breath
Just take what is left

Now and Then

The faint tick tick tick of the clock's hand
Pressing the hours forward like writings on the sand
A gentle breeze to wash up a distant memory
Of unsaid words behind every gaze
A familiar touch
And the faintest of smiles
But with a blink, the memory is washed away
And the faint tick tick tick of the clock's hand
Now deafening in my ears
Once so clear but now a blurry memory
Like waking up from a dream
But now and then
When the tide calms
The distant memory will appear again

Falling

Maybe if I sat here
Played a song or two
These memories wouldn't hurt so much
A jagged pain and such
With every breath, it hurts to breathe
A shallow of ice
My pierced lungs
I am drowning
This heavyweight has become too much
The crushing of my heart
Who knew where to start
You didn't even notice
Until I fell apart

Would I

Would I be like this if my father had stayed
Would he have tucked me in at night
And said that there was no reason to be afraid
That there are no monsters under the bed
And that the closet is too small for the bogeyman
Would he have wiped away my tears when my little
heart hurt
And taught me to throw a punch when the big bullies
lurked
If I went back to when I was eight
Would he still see his little girl
Or has my vision been distorted
That he was never there at all

Seeds

A seed of bitterness had been planted deep within my
heart
I clawed and I dug as deep as I could
But black poison seeped between my fingers
The inkiness smeared across my face as I tried to wipe
away my tears
And as I tried to claw open my chest to take the
bitterness away
I ended up with a hole in the middle of my heart

Deception

Your whispered words of lies
Is the poison around my heart
With every sip I drink
I choke on your deception

Seasons

A decade ago where were you?
When the hot, dreadful days of summer sweat turned
into cooler, crisp autumn air
The last firework show leaving you breathless
We can stay up late drinking Rose and carving pumpkins
I'll press a secret to your lips
A lingering taste of strawberries
Could you bear one more?
Listening to the melodies of our favorite songs
You take my hand and spin me around
The echoes of our laughter dance around us
You spin me around again
Your kiss is as sweet as the wine
On a winter night, I find myself a little drunk in love

Void

And when my hand reached out for yours
I was met with the emptiness
And through my tears
I was standing in what remained of your shadow

Afterthought

I long waited for the day when I did not need your
validation
Where my existence felt valued
But as the months have turned into years
Nothing has changed
And to my despair
I am, but an Afterthought

Winter

Why do I have such dreams?
The warmth of your voice calling out my name
Your brown eyes are drawn to mine
We dance in the middle of a starburst sunset
A dream within a dream
Don't wake me up
But from a sweet kiss to a hardened touch
You fade away
Like a misty morning
My sky turns grey
The phone goes silent
Not even an "I love you"

Memories

It's nothing like I thought it would be
The late-night tears
The heavy heart in the early mornings
There are no sweet words of affection
Or the I miss you when the day was long
It's a brief glance as if we were strangers
And the echos of what was

Lost

The closer I get to this place that we call home
The heavier the weight in my pitted stomach feels
Because this place is an empty reminder of what we lost
Us

Pinky Swear

Pinky promise that one day we'll meet again
Even though we broke each other's hearts
That you got lost to your demons
And I to my sorrows
That even though we may never be again
That when we die, our souls will move on to find one
another
That our love will forgive our sins
And pinky promise me that when we finally do meet
again
We will learn to love

Reflection

I am not perfect nor do I try to be
Through these hazel eyes and deep scars
There is a beautiful, four-eyed little girl to see
With dimples in her cheeks and a smile that travels far
She took the world head-on
Though it became heavy
She never imagined it would make her strong
She is both soft and hard
Light and darkness
If only she could see
That all she ever needed to be
Was herself